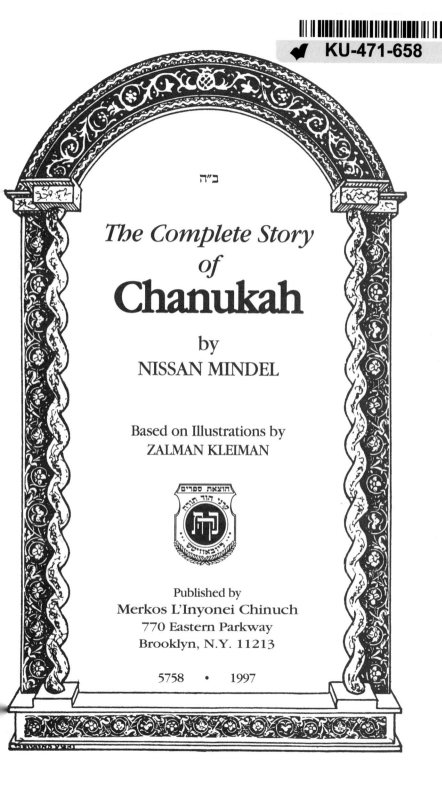

ב״ה

The Complete Story
of
Chanukah

by
NISSAN MINDEL

Based on Illustrations by
ZALMAN KLEIMAN

Published by
Merkos L'Inyonei Chinuch
770 Eastern Parkway
Brooklyn, N.Y. 11213

5758 • 1997

THE COMPLETE STORY OF CHANUKAH
Thirteenth Printing—New Revised Edition
Copyright © 1997 by

MERKOS L'INYONEI CHINUCH
770 Eastern Parkway • Brooklyn, N.Y. 11213
Tel: 718-774-4000 • Fax: 718-774-2718

ORDERS:
291 Kingston Avenue • Brooklyn, New York 11213
Tel: 718-778-0226 • Fax: 718-778-4148 • merkos@chabad.org

ISBN: 0-8266-0318-1

Manufactured in the United States of America

TABLE OF CONTENTS

The History of Chanukah

Tales of the Chanukah Lights

Supplement

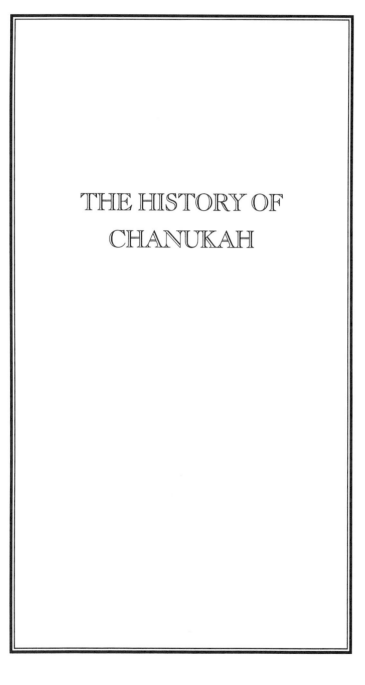

THE HISTORY OF
CHANUKAH

THE HISTORY OF CHANUKAH

UNDER SYRIAN RULE

More than 2000 years ago there was a time when the land of Israel was part of the Syrian Empire, dominated by Syrian rulers of the dynasty of the Seleucids.

In order to relate the story that led up to Chanukah, we shall start with Antiochus III, the King of Syria.* He had waged war with King Ptolemy of Egypt over the possession of the Land of Israel. Antiochus III was victorious and the Land of Israel was annexed to his empire. At the beginning of his reign he was favorably disposed toward the Jews and accorded them some privileges. Later on, however, when he was beaten by the Romans and compelled to pay heavy taxes, the burden fell upon the various peoples of his empire who were forced to furnish the heavy gold that was required of him by the Romans. When Antiochus died, his son Seleucus IV took over, and further

---

* Reigned 3538–3574

7

oppressed the Jews.

Added to the troubles from the outside were the grave perils that threatened Judaism from within. The influence of the Hellenists (people who accepted idol-worship and the Syrian way of life) was increasing. Yochanan, the High Priest, foresaw the danger to Judaism from the penetration of Syrian-Greek influence into the Holy Land. For, in contrast to the ideal of outward beauty held by the Greeks and Syrians, Judaism emphasizes truth and moral purity, as commanded by G-d in the holy Torah. The Jewish people could never give up their faith in G-d and accept the idol-worship of the Syrians.

Yochanan was therefore opposed to any attempt on the part of the Jewish Hellenists to introduce Greek and Syrian customs into the land. The Hellenists hated him. One of them told the King's commissioner that in the treasury of the Temple there was a great deal of wealth.

The wealth in the treasury consisted of the contributions of "half a shekel" made by all adult Jews annually. That was given for the purpose of the sacrifices on the altar, as well as for fixing and improving the Temple building. Another part of the treasury consisted of orphans' funds which were deposited for them until they became of age. Seleucus needed money in order to pay the Romans. He sent his minister Helyodros to take the money from the treasury of the

Temple. In vain did Yochanan, the High Priest, beg him not to do it. Helyodros did not listen and entered the gate of the Temple. But suddenly, he became pale with fright. The next moment he fainted and fell to the ground. After Helyodros came to, he did not dare enter again.

THE "MADMAN"

A short time later, Seleucus was killed and his brother Antiochus IV began to reign over Syria.* He was a tyrant of a rash and impetuous nature, contemptuous of religion and of the feelings of others. He was called "Epiphanes," meaning "the gods' beloved." Several of the Syrian rulers received similar titles. But a historian of his time, Polebius, gave him the epithet Epimanes ("madman"), a title more suitable to the character of this harsh and cruel king.

Desiring to unify his kingdom through the medium of a common religion and culture, Antiochus tried to root out the individualism of the Jews by suppressing all the Jewish Laws. He removed the righteous High Priest, Yochanan, from the Temple in Jerusalem, and in his place installed Yochanan's brother Joshua, who loved to call himself by the Greek name of Jason. For he was a member of the Hellenist party, and he used his high office to spread more and more of the Greek customs among the priesthood.

Joshua or Jason was later replaced by another man, Menelaus, who had promised the king that he would bring in more money than Jason did. When Yochanan,

---

* 3586.

the former High Priest, protested against the spread of the Hellenists' influence in the Holy Temple, the ruling High Priest hired murderers to assassinate him.

Antiochus was at that time engaged in a successful war against Egypt. But messengers from Rome arrived and commanded him to stop the war, and he had to yield. Meanwhile, in Jerusalem, a rumor spread that a serious accident, had befallen Antiochus. Thinking that he was dead, the people rebelled against Menelaus. The treacherous High Priest fled together with his friends.

THE MARTYRS

Antiochus returned from Egypt enraged by Roman interference with his ambitions. When he heard what had taken place in Jerusalem, he ordered his army to fall upon the Jews. Thousands of Jews were killed. Antiochus then enacted a series of harsh decrees against the Jews. Jewish worship was forbidden; the scrolls of the Law were confiscated and burned. Sabbath rest, circumcision and the dietary laws were prohibited under penalty of death. Even one of the respected elders of that generation, Rabbi Eliezer, a man of 90, was ordered by the servants of Antiochus to eat pork so that others would do the same. When he refused they suggested to him that he pick up the meat to his lips to appear to be eating. But Rabbi Eliezer refused to do even that and was put to death.

There were thousands of others who likewise sacrificed their lives. The famous story of Hannah and her seven children happened at that time.

Antiochus's men went from town to town and from village to village to force the inhabitants to worship pagan gods. Only one refuge area remained and that was the hills of Judea with their caves. But even there did the Syrians pursue the faithful Jews, and many a Jew died a martyr's death.

MATTITYAHU

One day the henchmen of Antiochus arrived in the village of Modin where Mattityahu, the old priest, lived. The Syrian officer built an altar in the marketplace of the village and demanded that Mattityahu offer sacrifices to the Greek gods. Mattityahu replied, "I, my sons and my brothers are determined to remain loyal to the covenant which our G-d made with our ancestors!"

Thereupon, a Hellenistic Jew approached the altar to offer a sacrifice. Mattityahu grabbed his sword and killed him, and his sons and friends fell upon the Syrian officers and men. They killed many of them and chased the rest away. They then destroyed the altar.

Mattityahu knew that Antiochus would be enraged when he heard what had happened. He would certainly send an expedition to punish him and his followers. Mattityahu, therefore, left the village of Modin and fled together with his sons and friends to the hills of Judea.

All loyal and courageous Jews joined them. They formed legions and from time to time they left their hiding places to fall upon enemy detachments and outposts, and to destroy the pagan altars that were built by order of Antiochus.

THE MACCABEES

Before his death, Mattityahu called his sons together and urged them to continue to fight in defense of G-d's Torah. He asked them to follow the counsel of their brother Shimon the Wise. In waging warfare, he said, their leader should be Yehuda the Strong. Yehuda was called "Maccabee," a word composed of the initial letters of the four Hebrew

words *Mi Komocho Bo'eilim Hashem*, "Who is like unto Thee, O G-d."

Antiochus sent his General Apolonius to wipe out Yehuda and his followers, the Maccabees. Though greater in number and equipment than their adversaries, the Syrians were defeated by the Maccabees. Antiochus sent out another expedition which also was defeated. He realized that only by sending a powerful army could he hope to defeat Yehuda and his brave fighting men.

An army consisting of more than 40,000 men swept the land under the leadership of two commanders, Nicanor and Gorgiash. When Yehuda and his brothers heard of that, they exclaimed: "Let us fight unto death in defense of our souls and our Temple!" The people assembled in Mitzpah, where Samuel, the prophet of old, had offered prayers to G-d. After a series of battles the war was won.

The Dedication

Now the Maccabees returned to Jerusalem to liberate it. They entered the Temple and cleared it of the idols placed there by the Syrian vandals. Yehuda and his followers built a new altar, which he dedicated on the twenty-fifth of the month of *Kislev,* in the year 3622.

Since the golden Menorah had been stolen by the Syrians, the Maccabees now made one of cheaper metal. When they wanted to light it, they found only a small cruse of pure olive oil bearing the seal of the High Priest Yochanan. It was sufficient to light only for one day. By a miracle of G-d, it continued to burn for eight days, till new oil was made available. That miracle proved that G-d had again taken His people under His protection. In memory of this, our sages appointed these eight days for annual thanksgiving and for lighting candles.

TALES OF THE
CHANUKAH LIGHTS

TALES OF THE CHANUKAH LIGHTS

The Chanukah lamp was kindled, shedding its faint light in the brilliantly lit sitting-room. It was a happy occasion for father to spend half an hour in the company of his children, playing the Chanukah dreidle. There was an air of festivity in the house, but so engrossed were the players in the game that the poor Chanukah light was all but forgotten.

The excitement grew as the *dreidle* spun round and fell, now with the *shin* up, calling for a 'put,' now with the *gimmel* up, bringing a 'take all' to the happy winner.

Little Chaim grew tired of the game and went up to look at the fascinating Chanukah light. He drew up a chair and sat down, gazing at the little flame with his eager blue eyes.

The tiny flame flickered and made a curtsy. "Good Chanukah!" the Chanukah Light said.

Little Chaim was so startled that he could only nod in acknowledgment. "I didn't know Chanukah Lights could talk," he said.

"Oh yes, Chanukah Lights can talk, and can tell

wonderful stories," the little flame replied. "Few children, I am sorry to say, know it. But I am glad you came to look me up. I was beginning to feel neglected. After all, I come but once a year, together with my seven little sisters, and surely we deserve some attention and hospitality."

"But we mustn't make any practical use of your light," Chaim said in self defense. "You are just to be looked at and pondered on!"

"I am glad you know that. But that is exactly the reason why you should sit next to me and keep me company, and listen to my story. I have such a wonderful story to tell you. Do you want to hear it?"

"I certainly do," little Chaim said expectantly.

The Story of the
First Chanukah Light

Many years ago, began the First Chanukah Light, the Jews lived in the Land of Israel. They had no king at that time, for their king was G-d, the King of kings. Unfortunately many Jews stopped serving G-d, and so they soon found themselves in the servitude of a human king. But he was not human at all, for he was a tyrant, and very, very cruel. His name was Antiochus, and he reigned in the neighboring land of Syria. So powerful was he, that no one could stop him from doing the most wicked things. Antiochus decided to make all Jews worship idols. He sent officers and soldiers throughout the Land of Israel to en-force the laws and customs of his land. The Jews were forbidden to worship G-d in their own way, or keep any other of their most sacred customs and laws. The Holy Temple in Jerusalem was defiled and stripped of its beautiful sacred golden vessels. Any one who dared to disobey the king was immediately put to death.

Days of terror and persecution followed. Then the Jews realized that their own wrongdoing had brought the trouble upon them. They began to mend their ways, and were resolved to die rather than give up their religion. Even little boys like you cheerfully faced cruel death and scorned a life of luxury as a heathen. Then G-d said, "My children have now suffered enough. I will rescue them!"

It was an old man, frail in body but a giant in spirit, who first raised the banner of revolt against the all-powerful king Antiochus. His name was Mattityahu the Hasmonean.

In the little peaceful village of Modin, Mattityahu lived with his five sons. When the king's officer with a company of men came to his village to force the Jews to worship idols, old Mattityahu grabbed the officer's sword and slew him. He called upon his sons and brethren to follow his example, and they pounced upon the vandals and slew most of them. The rest fled in terror to tell the king.

Old Mattityahu with his faithful followers withdrew to the hills. From there Mattityahu sent a message to all his brethren: "Let all faithful to G-d follow me!" and the band of followers who were ready to offer their lives for their faith grew daily.

One day Mattityahu gathered his friends around him, and said to them: "I feel that my last day is drawing near. Let my son Yehuda lead you to victory against the enemies of G-d. Though you may be greatly outnumbered, despair not, and put your faith in G-d. Remember our father Abraham who preferred to be thrown into the burning furnace rather than be unfaithful to G-d! Remember also Pinchas who risked his life for the sanctification of G-d's name! Remember Eliyahu the Prophet who stood up alone against the false prophets! He who answered them in their hour of peril shall answer you now. Fear not, but put your faith in G-d. G-d bless you and watch over you."

Soon after, Mattityahu passed away, sadly mourned by all Jews. The Jews now looked to Yehuda Maccabee to lead and guide them, and Yehuda was determined to live up to the reputation of his priestly family.

The Chanukah Light paused. The oil had run low, but the little flame struggled, almost desperately. "My time is up" she said. "Please be sure to be with us tomorrow. Happy Chanukah!"

The Story of the
Second Chanukah Light

The following day was Friday, and little Chaim washed early and changed for Shabbat, so he could be with the Chanukah Lights the moment they were kindled. He watched his father light the Chanukah Lights and then he watched his mother light the Shabbat candles. Now Chaim drew up a chair and sat down to accompany the Chanukah Lights.

Sure enough, he could hear the familiar voice of the First Light: "Good Shabbos and Happy Chanukah! I am glad to see you again. This is my younger sister. Say 'Hello' to the little boy."

"Hello," the Second Light said, making a graceful curtsy. "I know a wonderful story. Would you like to hear it?"

"I most certainly do," replied little Chaim. "Please, do tell it to me."

"Well," the Second Chanukah Light began, "Yehuda Maccabee led that little band of faithful Jews from victory to victory. Do you know what "guerilla warfare" is? It's the kind of war that a small number of people wages against big odds. Yehuda and his men did just that. Hiding in caves or lying in ambush, they would suddenly attack the enemy from the rear, or in the middle of the night. Although greatly outnumbered, they succeeded in routing the enemy every time.

Antiochus was bursting with rage. He sent one big army after another to capture Yehuda and destroy his followers, but each time his generals failed. Finally Antiochus sent his best general, Lysias, with a huge army of infantry and cavalry and armored chariots.

Yehuda addressed his handful of brave warriors: "Today we are put to our greatest test," he said. "But have no fear, for it isn't our weapons that defeated the enemy in the past, but our faith in G-d. They come in chariots and rely upon their might, but we come in the name of G-d and He will fight on our side."

Calling unto G-d and sounding their trumpets, Yehuda and his valiant followers flung themselves upon the enemy. Seeing Yehuda at the head of his men, looking like an angel of G-d, the Syrian warriors became terrified. Their whole army was thrown into terrible confusion, and they began to fight one another. Those who escaped the sword took to their heels, hotly pursued by Yehuda and his men.

It was a wonderful miracle indeed, and the victory was complete and overwhelming. Yehuda's first thought was to free Jerusalem and dedicate the Holy Temple, so that the Jews could once again worship G-d in peace and security.

When the goal was finally achieved and Yehuda, at

the head of his men, entered the Holy Temple, it was a sorry sight that met their eyes. Everything had been defiled and desecrated by the vandals. For a moment the spirit of triumph deserted them, and they stood there motionless, tears streaming down their cheeks.

"No time for grief!" Yehuda called. "Let's clean up and dedicate our Holy Temple! Everybody get busy!"

"Now we shall light the Menorah with its seven lights!" Yehuda announced when the Temple had been thoroughly cleansed. But alas! There was no pure, sacred olive oil to light it with, for everything had been defiled by the enemy. Searching again and again, they finally discovered one little cruse of oil that still bore the seal of the High Priest. Chanting Psalms to G-d for their deliverance, they kindled the Menorah and dedicated the Holy Temple in the year 3622 after Creation.

It was on the 25th of *Kislev*, the very day the Temple had been desecrated by the enemy, that the Dedication of the Temple was celebrated. But that was not all. Wonder of wonders! The little oil that was expected to last but one day lasted eight days, until new olive oil could be prepared for the Menorah. Here was a clear demonstration that G-d's miracles were beyond human understanding.

"This is where my part of the story ends," said the candle. "Tomorrow my younger sister will tell you another story of heroism. Now, you run along to *Shul* and be sure to be with us again tomorrow."

The Story of the
Third Chanukah Light

I mmediately after greeting little Chaim on the following evening, the Third Light began:

I'm going to tell you about Yehuda's younger brother Elazar.

The wicked Antiochus died, and his son Eopater became king of Syria. Eopater was no better than his father. He hired the biggest army for those days. It was composed of one hundred thousand infantry men, twenty thousand horsemen, and thirty-two trained war elephants. They all had armor and helmets and were veterans of previous wars. When the sun rose and shone upon the glittering array of armor, the reflected light dazzled the eye for miles around.

Determined to fight on to the last man, Yehuda

and his valiant warriors attacked the enemy, but not before they had prayed to G-d to help them in their holy cause.

It was a desperate battle, but Yehuda and his men fought on bravely. They destroyed one battalion after another, but there seemed no end to the swarming mass of the enemy. Suddenly Elazar noticed a war-elephant that was more elaborately decorated than the others, and heavily guarded. "There the king must be riding," thought Elazar. "If I kill him the victory will be ours." With no thought for his own life, Elazar rushed in the direction of the elephant. He fought his way through the guard, killing right and left, until he reached the decorated elephant. Elazar slew the elephant and its distinguished rider. But here the heroic Elazar also lost his life, caught beneath the crushing weight of the elephant as the huge beast collapsed from its wounds.

But it was not the king whom Elazar had killed but one of his top generals; nevertheless, Elazar's act of bravery inspired his brethren and they fought on grim-

ly. The odds were too heavily against them, however, and they found themselves in grave danger.

Suddenly a messenger brought news to the king of an uprising back in his own land. His son was attempting to overthrow him. Antiochus Eopater decided to call off this battle and make peace with Yehuda. Thus the Land of Israel was once again saved at the very moment when all seemed lost.

"That's all for the present," concluded the Third Chanukah Light, "Happy Chanukah!"

The Story of the
Fourth Chanukah Light

Four little flames flickered in the Chanukah Lamp. All of them curtsied and greeted little Chaim. Without losing any time, the Fourth Chanukah Light began her story:

Many battles were fought and won by Yehuda and his followers, but in one of the battles brave Yehuda fell. All Israel mourned the death of their hero. They then turned to his brother Yonatan for leadership.

Fortunately for the Jews, there was again trouble in Syria. Demetrius who was king of Syria at that time, was challenged by his rival, Alexander. Now Demetrius did not love Yonatan, and feared him. But even more did he fear his rival Alexander. So Demetrius decided to win Yonatan over to his side. He sent messengers asking Yonatan to forget the old grievances and become his friend.

Alexander met this move by sending Yonatan a golden crown and kingly robes with a message of friendship, saying that he would be glad to see him the High Priest and king of the Jews.

Yonatan sided with Alexander, for he knew that Demetrius was treacherous and was not to be trusted. When Alexander and Demetrius met on the battle-field, Demetrius fell in battle and Alexander triumphed. Alexander celebrated his victory in the town of Acco and invited King Ptolemy of Egypt and Yonatan to take part in the festivities. Yonatan was accorded royal honors.

Some years passed, and again a new king reigned in Syria. There was so much rivalry and treachery among the Syrians that they changed kings often. But in the meantime Yonatan reigned in the Land of Israel in a true spirit of justice and love. He was also the High Priest, being the grandson of Yochanan the High Priest. All Jews loved and honored him.

Now one of the trusted men of the king of Syria was a man called Triphon. Triphon wanted to murder the king and then proclaim himself king. Knowing that

Yonatan would avenge such treachery, he made up his mind to get rid of him. So Triphon made a party one day, and invited Yonatan. Yonatan did not suspect the trap Triphon had for him. When Yonatan was left unguarded, Triphon took him prisoner.

The Chanukah Light sighed as a shiny tear, like a pearl, rolled down Chaim's cheek.

"I am sorry my story has such a sad ending," said the Fourth Chanukah Light, "but my time is up. Tomorrow you will hear a more cheerful story. So long!"

The Story of the
Fifth Chanukah Light

Five little flames fluttered in the Chanukah Lamp. They all curtsied and greeted little Chaim with a hearty "Happy Chanukah!" The Fifth Light, shining more brightly than the others, began her story:

Now there was only one left of the five brave sons of Mattityahu. Yehuda, Elazar, Yochanan and Yonatan had all given their lives for their people. It was Shimon's turn to take over the leadership. All the people of Israel implored him to become their leader and High Priest, promising to follow him even as they followed his brothers.

The Land of Israel was still surrounded by many enemies, and Shimon had to fight many battles before he succeeded in freeing the country of all enemies within and without.

On the third anniversary of Shimon's leadership, all the elders and nobles of Israel gathered in Jerusalem to do honor to their beloved High Priest. They offered thanksgiving to G-d for delivering them from all their enemies. Amid great cheering and jubilation they proclaimed Shimon Prince of Israel and High Priest. All the people pledged their allegiance to him and his family. On bronze tablets the brave deeds of Mattityahu and his sons were then recorded, and the tablets were placed upon the columns supporting the balconies of the Holy Temple. Similar tablets were presented to Shimon as a token of everlasting love and gratitude.

Once again the Jews lived happily in their own land, free to worship G-d in peace and security. And every year, on the 25th day of *Kislev,* they celebrated the festival of Chanukah by kindling the Chanukah Lights, and telling their children of G-d's wonderful miracles.

The Story of the
Sixth Chanukah Light

The Sixth Chanukah Light flickered and curtsied and told her story:

My story will take you many years from those days of Chanukah under the Hasmoneans, for I am going to bring you back to our times, sad and tragic though they are. Once again, a cruel tyrant, even more cruel than Antiochus, declared an open war against our people and threatened to extinguish the light of our Torah.

My story takes you back to the early days of the Second World War, when Hitler's armies were drunk with conquest. My story takes you to a miserable place, a place unfit for human beings, a place which will always be spoken of with horror and aversion—a concentration camp.

This was a concentration camp in France, where many Jews had been herded and where they awaited an unknown fate.

It was into this concentration camp, the little Chanukah Light continued, that I was called to bring hope and courage to the suffering and despairing Jews.

There was a venerable man among them. He was a Rabbi. He was always on his feet going about from man to man, giving hope and solace to his brethren. But to bring hope to those despairing internees was quite a difficult matter.

Then Chanukah came.

For about a month before Chanukah, the Rabbi had been saving up some oil from his daily meals. He collected this precious oil drop by drop, and by Chanukah, he had enough of it to be able to fulfill the cherished *mitzvah* of kindling the Chanukah Lights. He managed to obtain a raw-carrot from the kitchen and cut out in it a little cup for the oil. From a corner of his coat he cut off a little piece for a wick. He now had a "Chanukah Lamp."

It was dark in the barracks where these poor Jews were confined, for their tormentors would not give them any light at night. In this silent darkness the venerable Rabbi's words seemed to come from nowhere, like a voice from heaven.

"My dear brethren," the Rabbi began, "tonight is Chanukah, the Festival of Lights, the festival that brings a message of hope to all Jews oppressed by tyrants like Antiochus. I am now going to light the Chanukah Lamp for all of us. Please listen carefully to the blessings."

Then, lighting the improvised Menorah, the Rabbi recited the three blessings over the first Chanukah Light. There were no tears in his eyes, and his voice rang with solemn hope and courage coming from the very bottom of his heart:

"My brethren," the Rabbi continued, while the little flame threw a dim light in the barracks. He could barely discern the sad faces of the internees but he knew there were tears in many eyes, and a stifled sob here and there confirmed this.

"Tonight," the Rabbi said, "is not a time for despair. Look at this little flame and try to understand what it signifies. When Aaron was about to kindle the

Menorah in the *Mishkan* (Sanctuary), G-d made a promise to him: that although the Menorah of the Temple might be put out for a time, when Israel turned away from Him, there would be a light that would always be kindled. This light would be kindled in the dark night and would bring light and hope to His children in their darkest hours. These lights were to be the Chanukah Lights.

"Let us, therefore, not despair, but pray to G-d to deliver us from the hands of our tormentors, so that we may live to rekindle the lights again next year in our Holy Land!"

Here the little flame paused, but young Chaim wanted to know what happened to those internees, and the little Chanukah Light continued:

Those were the more fortunate victims of Hitler. They had the good fortune to be regarded by him as "enemy aliens" and were held for exchange for German prisoners. After the Rabbi kindled the Sixth Chanukah Light, they received the happy news that they would be exchanged for German prisoners and sent to America. To this day they celebrate Chanukah with special joy because it is also the anniversary of their liberation. I must go and visit them at once. So long, my good little boy. I'll see you tomorrow!

The Story of the
Seventh Chanukah Light

Seven little flames fluttered in the Chanukah Lamp and all curtsied and greeted little Chaim with a hearty "Happy Chanukah!" The Seventh Light, shining more brightly than the others, began her story:

Do you know, my boy, that in the Holy Temple, the Golden Menorah had only seven lights, as many as you see tonight? That is why we do not have candlesticks of seven lamps, because we must not imitate the sacred vessels of the Holy Temple.

Now I see you are curious to know something more about the Menorah that stood in the Holy Temple. So I will tell you about that tonight:

You surely remember what you learned in Yeshivah about the Menorah, that it was beaten out of pure gold with a central shaft and six branches, three on each side, making up seven lamps in all. On top of each of the branches there was a cup. Each branch was further decorated with beautiful almond blossoms and knops, all made of that one piece of gold. It was a wonderful work of art. Even the great Moses found it difficult to grasp the instructions which G-d gave him verbally, and so G-d constructed the Menorah!

Only the purest of olive oils was used for the

Menorah. Do you know how it was prepared? Well, to begin with, no ordinary olives were used for the oil of the Menorah. Preference was first of all given to the oil of the olives growing around the city of Tekoa. No, not Tokyo, my boy, good heavens, no! Tekoa is a town in the Holy Land of Israel, where the Prophet Amos used to live. This town was located in the province belonging to the Tribe of Asher, whom Yaakov blessed with the words: "Asher's bread shall be fat and he shall yield royal dainties" (Gen. 49:20). The olives had to be grown on virgin soil which had not been artificially manured or irrigated. The olives had to be ripe and fresh from the tree, and only the first drops gently squeezed out from such choice olives could be used for the Menorah!

Every morning a special Priest, upon whom the duty and privilege of trimming and lighting the candle-stick for that day had been bestowed by lot, would reverently approach the Menorah. He would invariably find the western lamp burning, while the other six lamps of the Menorah had burnt out. This was a wonderful miracle that occurred every day, for while all seven lamps of the Menorah received an equal quantity of oil, sufficient only to last overnight, all the lamps did burn out overnight, while the western lamp still burned into the afternoon, when the Menorah was rekindled from that western lamp. This miracle showed that G-d's presence (the *Shechina*) was in the midst of Israel!

It was this sacred Menorah that the wicked
Antiochus defiled. He was able to do so only after the
Jews had forsaken the Torah and turned to Greek culture and idols instead. When the Jews turned away
from G-d, G-d turned away from them, and the light of
the Menorah was extinguished. However, when the
Jews rallied and returned to G-d wholeheartedly under
the guidance of the priestly family of Mattityahu and
his brave sons, G-d showed them again that His
Presence was among them. For, as you know, they
found only one little cruse of oil which had enough oil
for only one day, and by the miracle of G-d the little
quantity of oil in the Menorah lasted for eight days
until new, pure olive oil could be prepared.

This Menorah was one of the proudest and most
treasured articles among the spoils, Titus the Roman
general, took with him after he destroyed the Temple
many years later. So proud was he of his conquest of
the Land of Israel, the destruction of our Holy Temple
and especially the capture of our sacred Menorah, that
when a triumphal arch was built for him—the "Arch of
Titus"—a Menorah was very conspicuously depicted.
The cruel Titus thought that he had forever conquered
our people and extinguished its life. But he, like many
others of his kind, was wrong. Israel lived on and out-
lived his vast empire, for every Jew kindled within him
the light of the Torah. Every Jew became a walking
Menorah in an age of darkness.

By the time the Seventh Chanukah Light conclud-

ed her story, the others had already bade farewell to little Chaim. The Seventh Light too waved a final *au revoir*, but Chaim still remained sitting by the Chanukah Lamp, his blue eyes fixed on it. He was thinking... .

The Story of the
Eighth Chanukah Light

"We are all here now," cried out the Eighth Chanukah Light as soon as little Chaim found himself alone with the Chanukah Lamp, his brothers and sisters having gone off to play dreidle again. "This is our last night with you, dear little boy. Soon we'll have to bid you farewell until next year."

The Eighth Chanukah Light continued:

Do you know that it was not by accident that Chanukah occurred on the 25th of *Kislev*? I need hardly tell you that nothing happens by accident... The 25th day of *Kislev* first became important more than a thousand years before the "Miracle of Chanukah." It was on that day that the building of the *Mishkan* in the desert was completed-barely nine months after the children of Israel had been liberated from Egypt. At that time, however, G-d postponed the dedication of the *Mishkan* until the first of *Nissan*. "G-d does not withhold the reward of any creature," our Sages say. So G-d promised the 25th of *Kislev* that it would have its reward. When King Solomon concluded building the Holy Temple in the year 2935, the dedication took place on *Succot*, and the 25th of *Kislev* again had to bide time. The Second Temple was built and dedicated, but again the 25th of *Kislev* was left out. Finally,

the reward came when Yehuda Maccabee dedicated
the Temple after it had been defiled by the wicked
Antiochus, and the 25th of *Kislev* became an anniversary never to be forgotten.

"Trust G-d to grant adequate reward as surely as
He punishes for wrongdoing."

After a little pause, the Chanukah Light continued:

"Over the years we have often had a very difficult
task. Our people have suffered untold misery and pain,
have offered uncounted sacrifices for the sanctification
of G-d's name. Even in the darkest of all nights for our
people, we, the little Chanukah Lights, have brought a
ray of hope, heralding the dawn of a new day, a day
brighter than ever. Remember Rabbi Akiva and his
friends visiting the ruins of the Holy Temple?

Everybody wept but Akiva. "If the words of retribution with which our prophets admonished us came true, how much more so will their words of solace, their promise of survival and ultimate triumph!" Akiva said to his friends, and they wiped their tears and said, "Akiva, you have comforted us."

Yes, my boy, you may be sure that G-d does not withhold the reward of any creature, and our people will be rewarded, amply. The words, of our Prophet Isaiah will surely be fulfilled—we shall be "the light of the nations" and by our light the nations of the world will live in peace and happiness. For these are his words: "When darkness will cover the earth, and gross darkness the peoples-then G-d will shine upon you, and His glory will be seen upon you. And nations shall walk by your light, and kings by the brightness of your rising" (Isaiah 60:2,3).

* * *

"Well, little boy," all the Lights said in a chorus, "we hope you enjoyed our stories and talks. For more than 2000 years, we, tiny little Chanukah Lights, have come and gone, year after year, bringing with us tales of bravery and self-sacrifice in the cause of the Torah. You wouldn't think we are so old, would you? But we never grow old. We are timeless, and our message is timeless. Many a light have we kindled in Jewish hearts, and Jewish homes."

"Thank you, dear Chanukah Lights," little Chaim

said gratefully. "I shall always remember your wonderful stories. I wish I were like those brave Hasmoneans!"

"You might try to be..." the Chanukah Lights answered. "And now we are sorry to part with you- until next year ... Happy Chanukah, dear Chaim!"

"Happy Chanukah!" Chaim replied. "I shall be eagerly looking forward to seeing you next year!"

"In rebuilt, sacred Jerusalem!" the Chanukah Lights added.

"In rebuilt, sacred Jerusalem!" Chaim repeated.

SUPPLEMENT

SERVICE OF KINDLING
CHANUKAH LIGHTS

קודם שמדליק מברך

בָּרוּךְ אַתָּה יְיָ, אֱלֹהֵינוּ מֶלֶךְ הָעוֹלָם, אֲשֶׁר
קִדְּשָׁנוּ בְּמִצְוֹתָיו, וְצִוָּנוּ ׃ לְהַדְלִיק
נֵר, חֲנֻכָּה ׃
בָּרוּךְ אַתָּה יְיָ, אֱלֹהֵינוּ מֶלֶךְ הָעוֹלָם, שֶׁעָשָׂה
נִסִּים לַאֲבוֹתֵינוּ, בַּיָּמִים הָהֵם בִּזְּמַן הַזֶּה ׃

Before kindling the lights, the following blessings are said:

Blessed are You, Lord our God, King of the
universe, who has sanctified us with His com-
mandments, and commanded us to kindle the
Chanukah Light.

Blessed are You, Lord our God, King of the
universe, who performed miracles for our forefathers in those days, at this time.

בלילה הראשון של חנוכה מברך גם שהחיינו

בָּרוּךְ אַתָּה יְיָ אֱלֹהֵינוּ מֶלֶךְ הָעוֹלָם, שֶׁהֶחֱיָנוּ
וְקִיְּמָנוּ וְהִגִּיעָנוּ לִזְּמַן הַזֶּה ׃

The following blessing is said only on the first evening (or lighting):

Blessed are You, Lord our God, King of the
universe, who has granted us life, sustained us,
and enabled us to reach this occasion.

אחר שידליק הנרות יאמר זה

הַנֵּרוֹת הַלָּלוּ אָנוּ מַדְלִיקִין , עַל הַתְּשׁוּעוֹת ,
וְעַל הַנִּסִּים , וְעַל הַנִּפְלָאוֹת , שֶׁעָשִׂיתָ
לַאֲבוֹתֵינוּ בַּיָּמִים הָהֵם בַּזְּמַן הַזֶּה , עַל יְדֵי כֹּהֲנֶיךָ
הַקְּדוֹשִׁים . וְכָל שְׁמוֹנַת יְמֵי חֲנֻכָּה , הַנֵּרוֹת הַלָּלוּ קֹדֶשׁ
הֵם , וְאֵין לָנוּ רְשׁוּת לְהִשְׁתַּמֵּשׁ בָּהֶן , אֶלָּא לִרְאוֹתָן
בִּלְבָד , כְּדֵי לְהוֹדוֹת וּלְהַלֵּל לְשִׁמְךָ הַגָּדוֹל , עַל נִסֶּיךָ
וְעַל נִפְלְאוֹתֶיךָ , וְעַל יְשׁוּעוֹתֶיךָ :

After kindling the lights the following is said:

We kindle these lights [to commemorate] the
saving acts, miracles and wonders which You
have performed for our forefathers, in those days
at this time, through Your holy *Kohanim*.
Throughout the eight days of Chanukah, these
lights are sacred, and we are not permitted to
make use of them, but only to look at them, in
order to offer thanks and praise to Your great
Name for Your miracles, for Your wonders and for
Your salvations.

SOME CHANUKAH LAWS TO REMEMBER

1. The Chanukah Lights must be kindled at night-fall on each of the eight nights of Chanukah.

2. On the first night of Chanukah one light is kindled, on the following night, two, the third night, three, and so on, so that on the eighth night of Chanukah eight lights are kindled (not including the *Shamesh*).

3. On the first night, before kindling the lights of Chanukah, three blessings are said (see previous page).

4. On the following nights, only the first two blessings are said.

5. The lights are kindled left to right, so that the additional light of each night is kindled first.

6. After the lights are kindled we say: *Haneirot Halalu*.

7. The Chanukah Lights must burn for at least half an hour each night. Before kindling the lights, make sure that there is enough oil (or if candles are used, that they are big enough) to last half an hour.

8. No use should be made of the light shed by the Chanukah candles, such as reading or working by their light.

9. On Friday eve, the Chanukah Lights are kindled before the *Shabbat* Lights. Additional oil (or larger candles) should be provided for the Chanukah Lights to make sure they will last half an hour after nightfall.

10. On Saturday night the Chanukah Lights are kindled after *Havdalah.*

11. The Chanukah Lights must also be kindled in the Synagogue, but these do not absolve one from kindling the Chanukah Lights at home (not even the one who kindled them in the synagogue).

12. In the Synagogue the Chanukah Lights are kindled between the Afternoon and Evening Prayers. On Saturday night they are kindled before *Havdalah.*

13. During all of Chanukah *Al Hanissim* is added in the *Shmoneh Esrei* and in Grace after Meals. Complete *Hallel* is recited after *Shmoneh Esrei* in the Morning prayer.

14. A portion of the Torah is read in the Synagogue during the daily morning prayers.

Note: *There are certain laws as to the place where the Chanukah Lamp should be placed before the lights are kindled. If unknown to you—consult an authority.*

A CHANUKAH MESSAGE

from the Lubavitcher Rebbe
Rabbi Menachem M. Schneerson
זצוקללה״ה נבג״מ זי״ע

Dear Friend:

The Chanukah Lights which are kindled in the darkness of night recall to our minds memories of the past: the war that the Hasmoneans waged against huge Syrian armies, their victory, the dedication of the Temple, the rekindling of the Menorah, the small quantity of oil that lasted for many days, and so on.

Let's picture ourselves members of the little band of Hasmoneans in those days. We are under the domination of a powerful Syrian king; many of our brethren have left us and accepted the idolatry and way of life of the enemy. But our leaders, the Hasmoneans, do not commence action by comparing numbers and weapons, and weighing our chances of victory. The Holy Temple has been invaded by a cruel enemy. The Torah and our faith are in grave danger. The enemy has trampled upon everything holy to us and is trying to force us to accept his way of life which is that of idol worship, injustice, and similar traits altogether foreign to us. There is but one thing for us to do—to adhere all the more closely to our religion and its precepts, and to fight against the enemy even if we have to die in this fight.

And wonder of wonder! The huge Syrian armies are beaten, the vast Syrian Empire is defeated, our victory is complete.

This chapter of our history has repeated itself frequently. We, as Jews, have always been outnumbered; many tyrants attempted to destroy us because of our faith. Sometimes they aimed their poisoned arrows at our bodies, sometimes at our souls, and, sad to say, many of our brethren have for one reason or another turned away from G-d and His Torah and tried to make life easier by accepting the rule of the conqueror.

In such times of distress we must always be like that faithful band of Hasmoneans, and remember that there is always a drop of "pure olive oil" hidden deep in the heart of every Jew, which, if kindled, bursts into a big flame. This drop of "pure olive oil" is the "Perpetual Light" that must and will pierce the darkness of our present night, until everyone of us will behold the fulfillment of the prophet's promise for our ultimate redemption and triumph. And as in the days of the Hasmoneans "the wicked will once again be conquered by the righteous, and the arrogant by those who follow G-d's laws, and our people Israel will have a great salvation."

With Chanukah Greetings,
RABBI MENACHEM M. SCHNEERSON